PLATFORM PAPERS

QUARTERLY ESSAYS ON THE PERFORMING ARTS

No. 29
October 2011

CURRENCY HOUSE

This publication has been printed on paper certified by the Programme for the Endorsement of Forest Certification (PEFC). PEFC is committed to sustainable forest management through third party forest certification of responsibly managed forests. For more info: www.pefc.org

Democracy versus Creativity

in Australian Classical Music

NICOLE CANHAM

PLATFORM PAPERS

Quarterly essays from Currency House Inc.

Editor: Dr John Golder, j.golder@unsw.edu.au

Currency House Inc. is a non-profit association and resource centre advocating the role of the performing arts in public life by research, debate and publication.

Postal address: PO Box 2270, Strawberry Hills, NSW 2012, Australia

Email: info@currencyhouse.org.au   Tel: (02) 9319 4953
Website: www.currencyhouse.org.au   Fax: (02) 9319 3649

Editorial Board: Katharine Brisbane AM, Michael Campbell, Dr John Golder, John McCallum, Martin Portus, Greig Tillotson

ISBN 978 0 9807982 8 9
ISSN 1449-583X
Typeset in 10.5 Arrus BT
Printed by Ligare Book Printers, Riverwood, NSW
Photo of Nicole Canham by Chris Canham.
This edition of Platform Papers is supported by the Sidney Myer Fund, Neil Armfield, David Marr, Joanna Murray-Smith, Martin Portus, Alan Seymour and other individual donors and advisers. To them and to all our supporters Currency House extends sincere gratitude.

SIDNEY MYER FUND

Contents

AVAILABILITY *Platform Papers*, quarterly essays on the performing arts, is published every January, April, July and October and is available through bookshops or by subscription. For order form, see page 56.

LETTERS Currency House invites readers to submit letters of 400–1,000 words in response to the essays. Letters should be emailed to the Editor at info@currencyhouse.org.au or posted to Currency House at PO Box 2270, Strawberry Hills, NSW 2012, Australia. To be considered for the next issue, the letters must be received by 30 November.

CURRENCY HOUSE For membership details, see our website at: www.currencyhouse.org.au

Acknowledgements

Big thanks to my Polyartistry colleagues for being so talented, energetic and willing to try new things: David Finnigan, Sarah Kaur and Matthew Aberline, with Laura Scrivano, Carlos Lopez Charles and Applespiel. Special thanks to Clarity, John Davis, Drew Crawford, Dick Letts, Don Aitkin, Chris Canham, Matt Canham and Pam, Greg and Richard Whellum and to my music teachers, with whom I've spent many hours playing, practising and thinking about music: Nance Brennan, Suzanne Hewitt, Rachel Allen, Alan Vivian, Philippe Cuper and Susanne Powell. My thanks and gratitude to Lyndon Terracini and members of Opera Australia for their generous support of the Polyopera project. Thanks also to John Golder and Katharine Brisbane at Currency House for their thought-provoking questions and invitation to write this paper.

The author

Nicole Canham is a performing artist and artistic director whose work explores the understanding and interpretation of music and the place the arts hold in people's lives. She works in mainstream classical performance as a clarinettist and tarogato player, specialising in chamber music and collaborations with a range of artists from outside the world of music—theatre, film, photography, visual art and dance—exploring connections between artists and audiences. In 2009 she undertook an extended period of research overseas as a Churchill Fellow, investigating the positive impact of the arts in diverse communities, in Europe, the USA, Canada and Mexico.

After completing a Bachelor of Music Degree in Performance at the Australian National University School of Music, Nicole undertook post-graduate study with Philippe Cuper at the CNR de Versailles and obtained her *prix de perfectionnement*. With the quartet Clarity, she toured to Belgium, France and the UK. Since 2005 she has been a Move Records artist.

Recent work has included participation in Chamber Made Opera's performance and recording of Helen Gifford's *Exile*, launched as an i-pad application in late 2010, and residencies with new media artist Sarah Kaur at Punctum Live Arts in Castlemaine, Victoria, and at the Centro Nacional para la Musica y las Artes

Sonoras, Mexico; and with dancer/choreographer Nerida Matthaei at the Firkin Crane, Ireland. Other engagements have included performances at the UNAM Esceula Nacional de Musica Clarinet Festival, the 12 Nights Festival of electro-acoustic music, Miami, the Visiones Sonoras Festival, Morelia, concerts in Canberra, Melbourne, Paris, and with the Sydney Symphony Orchestra. Nicole is currently engaged in a major commissioning project of new works for tarogato.

As Artistic Director of the Canberra International Music Festival 2005–8, Nicole led the event through a period of significant growth and change, achieving a ten-fold increase in attendance over four years. The addition of an extensive program of new music and her commitment to providing quality arts experiences for young people were major additions to the Festival: her education program in 2008 provided concert experiences for 25 percent of the ACT's primary school children, featuring music by living Australian composers. Other hallmarks were site-specific programs for the National Film and Sound Archive, The National Gallery of Australia and Old Parliament House. The 2007 Festival received an Australian Classical Music State Award for most outstanding contribution by an organisation, and the 2008 Festival was a national finalist in the Australian Classical Music Awards. Nicole has worked as a consultant on programs for the Centenary of Canberra, the Museum of Australian Democracy and as a sessional lecturer at Monash University. She lives in Melbourne, and is a doctoral candidate at the University of Queensland.

Nicole's website is www.nicolecanham.com

Introduction

Those of us working in the classical music sector today tend to have a very limited understanding not only of the general public's relationship with their own creativity, but also of the impact this has on their potential interest in, and long-term appreciation of, the creativity of others. Which is a way of saying that none of our surveying and reporting and documentation for grant acquittals is really asking the essential question: Why don't you, or wouldn't you, come to our concert? Or if you were to come, what would you like to see/hear?

A further aspect of the problem, one that makes it widespread and difficult to contain within the scope of a short essay, is that it is in part generated by the attitude of the specialist or technocrat—both from a performance and an administrative standpoint. In our effort to have every note in tune and to make our classical art form organisations and artists more business-like and professional we seem to have become confused about when to use the eye and ear of the specialist, and when to ignore the specialist in order to tune into contemporary culture. The things we hold dear in our own art form differ markedly from those that are part and parcel of daily living in the twenty-first century. If we are genuinely anxious to nurture a meaningful relationship with a wider audience, we need to take the time to develop processes and practices that enable us to rejoin the rest of humanity and see whether we can share their intellectual and emotional headspace.

Classical music is good for us. The economic and social benefits of the El Sistema program in Venezuela are just one example of music being a great leveller, and a positive, contributing factor when trying to assist individuals in a variety of social circumstances to bring about significant personal change. Why might that be? Music-making and listening can inspire us to put aside our daily concerns and aspire to a way of living that is beyond the lowest level of Maslow's hierarchy of needs. All of these long-term, socially beneficial things are frequently cited when arts funding cuts are being discussed or when we are seeking money for our activities. Yet it seems that the classical music sector in Australia has been less successful in sharing our aspirations with as many Australians as we might like, and certainly not with as many as we might need if our healthy survival is to be guaranteed. We might be saying the words, but are we achieving those powerful moments of connection with our audiences so that they continue to grow? I'm not so sure. In their approach to this problem the 'makers' of Australian classical music are seriously lacking in the right kind of creativity. I became aware of this lack through my own work with many different people in the classical music world in the areas of performance and teaching, when working as a producer and artistic director of a festival, or when developing education programs, working in partnership with national institutions, assessing grant applications or having cultural-policy discussions at a state government level. I do not intend this as a criticism of the people I have encountered in my professional life—far from it. For the most part those working in classical music and the arts are dedicated, hard-working and passionate. What I do intend, and it is the essential purpose of this essay, is to ask some questions about the foundations of our approach to our work and the way in which we hold, develop and expand our conversation about classical music with the broader Australian public.

The reasons why many people dislike classical music, and new music in particular, are many: it's too long, boring, expensive, hard to understand, in a foreign language, only for old people ... Tired of the art taking the blame for what is really a people problem, I became interested in the way that we present what we do, the way that we work and interact with others, including audiences. My work as Artistic Director of the Canberra International Music Festival between 2005 and 2008 had been greatly informed by some administrative work I had done for Pro Musica, the festival's producer, at the 2004 festival. One of my tasks was to conduct the audience survey, and it was a highly illuminating experience to speak with a large number of passionate, classical music enthusiasts. I got to meet the people I would be working for in the following four festivals, but I also quickly understood which potential audiences were being left out.

What kinds of people are attracted to classical music? A classical-music audience member in Australia fits quite a specific profile—university-educated, reasonably well-off, fifty-plus. What kind of personality type is attracted to working in the area of classical music? Why have we structured our classical-music industry the way we have through our cultural-policy making? And to what extent do we reflect the reality of our contemporary Australian society and our national sense of identity? In particular, how responsive are we—are we able to be—towards our society? Can we be presenters of classical work and at the same time maintain the attitude of contemporary artists?

Australian society is comprised of many different nationalities. As Hugh Mackay revealed in his book *Advance Australia...Where?*:

> We are creating a society from the blending of people who have comeq here from nearly 200 different birthplaces around the world and that, right now, 50 percent of us were either born overseas or have at least one parent born overseas.[1]

In the world of classical music we have, until quite recently, had our eye firmly on what was happening in Europe as a measure of the worth of our work. This has changed significantly in the last half-century, as the infrastructure necessary for a thriving home-grown artistic landscape has been put in place: the establishment of many of our major festivals, the formation of the Australia Council, the building of performing arts spaces such as the Sydney Opera House. We find ourselves now with a high level of confidence as a nation, and, compared with many other countries in the world, a beautiful, affluent, safe and harmonious place in which to live and work. We may no longer need the European stamp of approval— but we do need, more than ever, the approval of the diverse and complex group of people that constitute our immediate community.

A question the classical-music sector is often asked goes something like this: If we were effectively engaging people in classical music, shouldn't the outcome of all our efforts be different? In the plethora of activities that involve the art form and the artist, administrators, stakeholders, sponsors and audiences, is there something we're all missing? In fact, one fundamental failure has been obvious for some time: either we have been slow to recognise the ways in which our classical art form is out of step with contemporary culture, or else we have recognised it and been unwilling to do much about it—or both. A lack of genuine interest in the wide cross-section of our social mix and their motivations when it comes to art and entertainment is a serious impediment to the development of new audiences.

There is no shortage of passion or creativity when it comes to our craft. The hallmarks of the art form include the importance of excellence and high levels of technical skill, formality of structure and rituals of performance. In the ideal world—the model we've been taught to desire and expect—there are clearly delineated roles for administrators, audiences, composers and performers. They make a landscape of specialists who have spent years honing their skills in a very particular field of endeavour. Long-standing traditions of practice condition and dictate our behaviour and expectations.

Certain aspects of our recent history influence us too, but it could be argued that our passion for classical music and for the preservation of its traditions has blinkered us and put limits on our agenda. We continue to be resistant to the need to take a wider view of the industry and our society. We also steadfastly refuse to assume the level of individual responsibility required for our art form to make a greater social and cultural impact on our immediate world. The general indifference to our efforts, and our struggle to survive and produce work to the standard of which we are capable, are as much problems of our own making as they are signs of the influence of government cultural policy, say, or a rapidly changing society, or a profile we might develop of the 'average' contemporary Australian.

What was surprising to me in the context of the Canberra International Music Festival, and the subsequent ten-fold increase in attendance that we achieved over four years, is that although it was a lot of work it wasn't actually that *difficult* to bring a whole new audience to the festival. We didn't try to convince people that classical and new music could be interesting, but we did spend a lot of time creating a wider range of opportunities and experiences within the program that enabled all those new people to see themselves as part of the festival.

One could come up with a list of other factors that might also have had a role in that significant period of growth and change. But it certainly has given me pause for thought as I attempt to reconcile the problems, as I perceive them, of the classical-music sector as a whole, and our apparent difficulty with working effectively and cohesively to build a thriving sector across the spectrum of our activities. Why shouldn't we be thriving? We have a terrific product.

Central to our seeking any kind of solution is the need to look first for a common reference point before we can begin to address our differences. For me this is creativity, the unique and individual spark we all possess. Better to harness our own creativity in new ways than continue to send a message crafted by and for those with other interests. I believe the way to a more vibrant future for classical music lies in collaborating to bring out the creativity in others. Accordingly, and from the perspective of a classical music insider who often feels like an outsider in her own art form, this essay looks at ways in which we might be more innovative together. In the process it presents some case studies of artists and organisations that are looking at new ways to give people engaging experiences of classical music.

To begin with, though, we might reflect briefly upon the Federal Government's policy statement of 1994, *Creative Nation*, written just a year before the world-wide web really took off, to see how we measure up, seventeen years on.

1

Creative Nation? The appreciator versus the creator

An initiative of Prime Minister Paul Keating, *Creative Nation* is a substantial document in which the arts in Australia are seen to offer great possibilities, and the cultural and creative industries to become not only major contributors to our economy, but also vehicles for all Australians to explore and express their identity. From the point of view of a classical musician it's also full of tension.

Essentially, it sets out with the idea that creators, or people working on that side of the creative realm—artists and arts administrators—must continue their efforts to create an economy based on creativity and ideas; become more professional and businesslike, more excellent, more recognised at home and abroad ... and at the same time be delivering this level of art to every Australian.

> To speak of Australian culture is to recognise our common heritage. It is to say that we share ideas, values, sentiments and traditions, and that we see in all the various manifestations of these what it means to be Australian. [...]
>
> Culture then, concerns identity—the identity of the nation, communities and individuals. We seek to preserve our culture because it is fundamental to our understanding of who we are. It is the name we go by, the house in which we live. Culture is that which gives us a sense of ourselves.[2]

To perform classical music at a consistently high standard requires natural talent, persistence, many years of training and the development of some specific ways of thinking. These include developing the ability to concentrate for long periods of time, to be able to determine quickly what information needs concentration and what is a distraction from the deep focus that has to be placed elsewhere. We devote lengthy periods of time to our music practice because it is inherently a difficult and complex task.

A wonderful classical music performance is this kind of 'small detail' thinking working at its best. It's also vastly different from the kind of thinking and perspective required to consider the needs of a larger group of people with diverse interests or the broader social context of our passion/work. And that's where things start to become tricky, because *Creative Nation* goes on to articulate a vision in which we are excellent at all the small-detail work that is fundamental to making high-quality, engaging musical performances— and at the same time are able to assess the value of our actions in the context of our society:

> Culture, therefore, also concerns self-expression and creativity [...] We recognise that the life of the nation and all our lives are richer for an environment in which art and ideas can flourish, and in which all can share in the enjoyment of them. With a cultural policy we recognise our responsibility to foster and preserve such an environment. We recognise that the ownership of a heritage and identity, and the means of self-expression and creativity, are essential human needs and essential to the health of society.
>
> Because culture reflects and serves both the collective and the individual need, because it at once assures us of who we are and inspires us with intimations of the heights we might reach, this cultural policy pursues the twin goals of democracy and excellence. It will make the arts and our intellectual and cultural life and heritage more accessible to all.[3]

Here are the horns of our dilemma. A cultural policy written by a public servant is going to express the notion of what constitutes excellence in classical music, and the way in which one might go about achieving it, very differently from one written by a classical musician, a practitioner.[4] *Creative Nation* is in many ways a Pollyanna-ish view of the way things might be in an ideal world, and not, on the whole, written from the perspective of the artist, although artists were obviously expected to play a major role in actioning what was outlined.

A further issue is that of democratic access to excellent art, proposed in *Creative Nation* as a key aspiration of culture in enabling us to develop our identity, as both individuals and as a nation, through the arts. This gives the appreciator a central role to play, and makes the government, as an arts patron by proxy, the representative of the broader Australian public. Classical musicians, on the other hand, might appreciate a very technically secure performance, excellent intonation, reliability, expression, or a range of other skills displayed in musicianship. Beyond ensuring that one understands basic onstage etiquette, the appreciation of the audience is not a strong focus in the formative years of a student's classical-music training. As a young clarinettist, I certainly have no memory of a lesson in which my teacher discussed the broader contemporary social context of the way in which I might choose to interpret a Brahms sonata. Perhaps that was a good thing: it's something in which most Australians have absolutely no interest.

There is another lingering question around notions of identity raised in *Creative Nation*—and that is the idea that it should work both ways. If those who work in classical music understand and identify themselves as specialists, then all that history, that repertoire and the rituals around performance are critical parts of our definition of ourselves as classical musicians, and not exponents of another style of music. The disciplines and attitudes which are rigidly maintained in order to interpret a musical text at a 'technically perfect/accurate standard' (often to the exclusion of many other artistic values including spontaneity, improvisation) are the foundation stones of our art form. Our identity as classical musicians is closely tied to behaviour that can be baffling to others. How many times have you been asked at a party if you can perform something from memory? And how many classically trained musicians would agree to perform despite their fear of making a mistake? How many can't play anything without music? Won't improvise or try to improvise? Our identity is shaped and formed by whatever we think it will take to achieve *excellence*.

This isn't the same as connection. So a cultural policy which puts the appreciator, who doesn't necessarily understand this behaviour or the reasons behind it, in the role of patron, and places the bureaucrat who represents them in direct opposition to the specialist classical musician.

Try to explain this or justify it and people's eyes glaze over—there are good reasons why people will express an interest in the arts but not choose to pursue such a career for themselves. It isn't a way of working or a lifestyle that suits everyone. What they might respect in the context of our choosing to become a professional classical musician, however, is the cherished Australian notion of the 'fair go', and the general consensus of what we believe democracy to be.

2

Equality versus merit

People often confuse democracy with equality, and the idea that one's success in work and life (however we choose to define it) has to do with merit—since we've worked so hard to create a level playing field for everyone.

By analogy, a meritocracy is like a fairly contested race in which all competitors start together and run over the same track, with victory and the spoils going to the swiftest. The Australian situation, in contrast, more closely resembles the case where a few competitors start one metre from the finishing line, a few more fifty metres back up the track, a larger group are further back hammering in their starting blocks, others are still changing in a crowded dressing room, while the remainder are at home under the impression that the race starts tomorrow... In a meritocracy only those with the appropriate mixture of natural ability and hard work will rise to the top and stay there. [...]

The principle of *equality of opportunity* does not, as is often implied, promise an equal opportunity for all to win the race, merely to start together. Of what possible use is this guarantee to a middle-aged heart patient with weak ankles lining up next to the current Olympic champion? The cruel joke practised on that mass of humanity by being granted

the opportunity to lose ingloriously to the able few
is heightened when it is realised that the rules of
the race, as well as its prizes, are determined by the
ruling elite.[5]

Without reading beyond the introduction to *Creative
Nation*, we can see some very big questions starting to
arise. Under this policy, the Government is essentially
saying to artists and arts organisations (including the
classical-music sector), 'We will support you to become
excellent, and to ensure that the widest possible range
of people have access to what you are doing.' While
telling the sector in quite a technocratic way that a
major pathway to the achievement of this is through
bureaucratic reform and administrative structures
with increased transparency and accountability, the
document makes it pretty clear where the responsibility
lies in terms of the democratic dissemination of the
work:

> The Commonwealth takes the view that
> responsibility for our creative life is shared, and that
> not least among those who must work to develop
> self-reliance and self-sufficiency are the artists and
> their agencies and audiences. Without endorsing
> the view that government support tends to stultify
> creative output, the Commonwealth Government
> is determined that our cultural development will be
> driven as far as possible by the creative energy of
> individuals, groups and communities.[6]

We in the classical community continue to use
practices and models of performance, education and
business that create significant barriers of access to
classical music for both artists and audiences. But one
might argue that with a document like *Creative Nation*
as the foundation of our cultural-policy thinking and

its influence on future cultural policies, we were set an extremely difficult task and required to use a set of tools that are counter-intuitive to our ways of thinking and working. It also needs to be pointed out that the effectiveness of this way of working is limited, and that we are experiencing the impact of this now.

Clearly, there are difficulties in attempting to apply concepts of equality and merit when it comes to both the arts and Australian society in general; inequality is alive and well, and there are many who would argue that it is necessary. Where we fail, however, is in forgetting to acknowledge the way in which that 'fair go' value has been applied to our way of looking at what we contribute to our society. There are many Australians who believe that our society *is* founded on the concept of equal opportunity for everyone and that one *does* succeed, or *not* succeed, in life according to the merit of one's deeds. It is not a very big step then for the average Australian to conclude that the difficulties we face in classical music are generated from within our sector and that our place on the edge of daily life is somehow deserved.

If we feel, or are perceived as being, set apart from mainstream Australia, it comes as much from situations of our own making as it does from the response of our fellow citizens—in itself, of course, a response, or lack of response, to what we contribute to the national conversation. There are two questions we might be asking ourselves here:

1. Is 'democratic access to the arts' simply a feel-good statement made in order to satisfy voters about the good intentions behind government expenditure of their taxpayer funds?

2. Or do we really mean and aspire to the idea that all Australians should, can and will have access to great art—in this case classical music?

Can the aspirations of the classical-music sector be ticked off in the acquittal process by some standard survey questions or other community-focussed questionnaire? If our cultural policy exists simply to satisfy the scrutiny of a sceptical voter, then we should carry on as we do without further reflection. Take the blue pill.

Or we could take the red pill, and see what it's like inside the Matrix ...

Tough love

The difficulty here, of course, is not simply a question of whether we really mean it when we say we'd like all Australians to have access to quality classical music. We are well behind our other art-form counterparts, including theatre, visual art and contemporary dance, when it comes to finding ways to maintain standards of excellence in performance while reaching new audiences. This has a lot to do with being stuck in the bind of valuing perfection over connection.

Why is this the case? From a classical musician's perspective the easiest part of *Creative Nation* to grasp is the value placed on excellence. However, the policy seems to imply that if we were 'more excellent' as a sector, then people would be able to have access to great art, and somehow everyone would come along and discover their identity—without really understanding that the attainment and maintenance of a level of excellence is a full-time job in itself.

Classical musicians spend much of their working life with their heads in the past rather than the present, or at the very least, with their heads in the music and not, as a general rule, thinking about the problems of society at large and what they might do about that armed with their violin or oboe. So perhaps we might find some consolation in the ideas of conservation, of restoration and of preservation? Classical music is, necessarily and unavoidably, a tradition in which we look to the past, or routinely refer to the past for interpretive ideas and methods of training, working and performance in order to interpret and perform music written by people who are now deceased. We continue to perform this music because it continues to speak to us, hundreds of years after it was written. Much of it was composed for specific occasions and events, supported or commissioned by royalty and or the wealthy upper classes. It was also often the popular music of its day (there are obvious exceptions like Stravinsky's Rite of Spring among many others—scandalous and derided at the time, and now considered a masterpiece), and this is reflected in the way the work of favourite composers has been preserved through study and performance over generations. From all round the world there has been handed down to us a rich catalogue of beautifully crafted music reflecting a wide range of styles, tastes and aesthetic possibilities.

Since it has not been possible to preserve all of the original context in which this music was created and performed, we endeavour to ensure that what we do in terms of performance is as faithful to the text as we can make it. Even though our contemporary music reflects many other influences, today we continue to perform the classical repertoire, with white gloves, seeking to present the work in stylistically appropriate ways, underpinned by knowledge of the history behind the music. Beyond the performance realm an industry of research and debate thrives on seeking lost manuscripts, creating new, more accurate editions of masterworks and unearthing further information about the ways in which these pieces came into being. It's a world of detailed and demanding accuracy, a world in which students learn for the most part through a process of being encouraged to strive for perfection in technical facility and accuracy, and in which the shaping of each piece of music comes with a heavy load of history. For the specialist all of this detail can be illuminating, revelatory, magical. But it's lost on many others.

How can I possibly summarise in a few short paragraphs the commitment I have made for more than two thirds of my life, immersed in the discovery and mastery of both instrument and repertoire not only from the perspective of a performer, but also as a custodian of a tradition of music? People who have never played an instrument, but imagine it must be a lot of fun, can hardly appreciate what is actually involved in being a professional classical musician.

Joseph Haydn seemed able successfully to balance the creative side of his work with non-musical duties. Appointed in 1757 by the Austrian aristocrat Count Morzin to the post of Kapellmeister, his contract insisted that, in addition to composing music and performing concerts at the request of his employer, see to the maintenance of instruments, the cataloguing of musical scores, and deliver lectures. In addition to keeping in mind all the details of Haydn's contract, more often than not we have to adopt the viewpoint of the elite athlete in order to even get a start in today's classical-music world. This means many hours of practice from a young age, at a time when our contemporaries are outside kicking around a soccer ball. It isn't for everyone and it requires first of all a love of music and a desperate need to play it. It also requires a high degree of control and personal discipline, which tends to attract a certain kind of personality. I'm not suggesting that we are all control freaks of some sort, but the world of classical music does create some precise expectations about how we need to behave in order to achieve any kind of recognition. Although the notion of a single kind of career path or area of artistic activity for the classical musician has been changing for some time, we are certainly in the minority—without many of the other benefits that we might draw upon if we were to identify ourselves as a community of rebels (also usually in the minority).

Seventeen years on, how might we measure the legacy of *Creative Nation*? Many of the structural and organisational reforms that it recommended have been successfully implemented. On the other hand, we have fallen well short of its aspiration that our whole society should enjoy all the art forms at a high standard of performance. In part this is because the nature of the industry reform outline fails to take into account the amount of time it takes to produce excellent work—or if it does, by believing that piling additional layers of structure and accountability would make us great at getting out there and sharing our work. That kind of shift doesn't simply require procedural reform; it requires deep, lasting and significant intellectual reform and lengthy debate about the fundamental values of the art form.

Additionally, the foundation laid for a sector approach to classical music through our cultural policy is fundamentally flawed: *Creative Nation* lays the responsibility for developing a healthy, lively and sustainable arts sector firmly at the feet of the people working in the sector, but the tools it suggests are inappropriate to the task of achieving the vision put forward. Perhaps the reason we have difficulty sustaining an effective and coherent debate in the classical music sector about what would be best for us all has to do with a sense that we've run out of ways of working with these tools. Everyone is doing everything they possibly can—but things aren't really getting that much better. We need a paradigm shift; a new way of viewing the world, and one in which we can achieve a much deeper and more sincere connection with other people. If our approach was working, classical music would be a lot more popular.

3

Cathedrals and casinos

I ♥ AC/DC

Not the least of our problems in inviting people to experience classical music is an inability to speak to them in an intelligible language: we talk in obscure, arcane terms to people who like listening to rock bands. Pause for a second to ask why that might be so. Can you imagine going to a rock band website and finding information about how to enjoy a rock concert? Or when to applaud? Or what to wear? The advantage that rock fans have over classical-music lovers is that they are free to say what it is that they love about their music without feeling the need to have spent years training in or learning about the subject. What's more, for rock fans that's perfectly acceptable. The powerful image projected by a rock band, what it might be like to be at one of their concerts, sets the tone for the kind of interaction you might have as one of their fans. As Anthony Bozza puts it:

> A rock-and-roll band is like a gang, a clan, or a family—often a dysfunctional one—that comes together to say something. Whether their message is revolutionary or nothing new at all matters just as much as—or as little as, or even less than—how they say it. In popular music, the message isn't simply in the words and music; the musicians are the message, too. They are representatives of the point of view, the opinions expressed, and the stories told in the music they create. Whether their image is manufactured, imposed, or an organic extension of the artist's or band's personality, it is their most powerful tool. As loud as their sound might be, their image will always be louder.[7]

Of course it's a good idea for people to be informed about what kind of experience they are about to have, and to be prepared—but so much of the classical music attitude seems to be about 'getting it right' even for audiences, rather than about having an amazing, connective experience that will leave people wanting more. Bozza goes on:

I don't care how personal the nature of the art form may be, a performance cannot exist in a vacuum. No performers play for themselves alone (though one might argue the case when it comes to mimes), because the essence of performance isn't just communication, it is connection. There are few human stories that haven't already been told and there are no human emotions that haven't been felt before in our two hundred thousand years on earth. Art and performance are creative retellings of our communal history, meant to be witnessed and consumed by an audience. Without a witness, a performance is practice and it has no meaning beyond the player's experience.[8]

The difference between what it takes to be excellent and what it takes to be loved is enormous. Our art form traditionally views excellence obtained over years of training and experience as the apex of achievement. It soars into the air like a cathedral spire, puncturing the skyline in a way that a skyscraper does not. Not only is the spire finer and more elegant, it represents values and attitudes that were fundamental to the fabric of daily life in times past. Our classical-music cultural policy, however, would have us generate the enthusiasm of the rock fan in our audiences, in order to justify our existence. So, how are we to make friends and fans in the world we currently inhabit?

Melbourne has a wonderful cafe culture. Take a walk down Chapel Street, and every second shop is a cafe or hole-in-the-wall-style restaurant. While you are walking, take note of which cafes are full and which are empty: it isn't uncommon to find two places next to each other, one full of people and the other maybe with only one or two customers. Perhaps it is the menu, or the brand of coffee, or the ambience—or perhaps it's just that people prefer to be somewhere else. If the menu of the empty Chapel Street cafe were nothing but classical music, how might we go about attracting some of our neighbours' customers? It's a matter of what we put on our menu and whether people want it.

A cathedral is a building that is full of symbolism. But no matter what building we look at, it will have symbolic meaning, referring to ideas and values beyond the utility value of the building as, say, a place for shelter or rest. People, like myself, who work in classical music often love being absorbed in these kinds of details. There is a level of subtlety, of shutting out the rest of the world while we take time to appreciate the sound of a note, or an interaction between instruments, that enables us to both lose, and at the same time deeply connect, not only with ourselves, but with ideas more beautiful than our daily concerns. A propensity to thoughtfulness and reflection are often required in order to appreciate the complexity of all this. People working in classical music are sold on this way of looking at the world and on a way of interacting with people that says, 'Let me help you get to know this cathedral.'

But we put so much effort into trying to keep the cathedral of classical music in pristine condition that we seem not to have noticed that, or else not asked ourselves why, most people are up the road. Or else we do notice, and quickly reassure ourselves by saying that they simply don't understand what it is that we are trying to do. Look at the beautiful workmanship, we say, listen to that passage or phrase, see the detail in that new production, what a wonderful program. We get further off the track when we start asking the people who *are* coming to the cathedral lots of questions about their age, the kind of music they like, what they would like to hear. If our current audience is too small, if all our complaints about not having enough freedom to program lesser-known music or new music are genuine, then it's not a larger audience that we need, but an entirely new one.

So where is everyone, and what are they currently interested in? Social commentator Hugh Mackay has written recently about the disengagement of many Australians in the aftermath of 9/11 and a general shift, away from the bigger, external problems that seemed too difficult to resolve, towards a more internal focus:

> Disengagement is easy to confuse with apathy, but it's a quite different thing. In the Dreamy Period, we might have been turning our backs on political and social issues that had the potential to darken our mood, but we were not apathetic: we had simply shifted focus from the big picture to the miniatures of our own lives. The issue was control. When so many issues seemed beyond our control, we began to concentrate instead on the things we could control, and there were plenty of contenders.[9]

A more internal focus makes us look to our immediate surroundings for comfort:

> [L]ifestyle programs came from nowhere to rate their socks off [...] In 2006, symbolically, Australia's No.1 bestseller was Spotless, a book of household cleaning hints.[10]

So up at the casino—that's where the majority of people are—the discussion, prompted by the most recent episodes of *The Block* and *Masterchef*, is all about home renovation, or else whether the blueberry cheesecake is too dry, or whether it might taste better with a raspberry coulis. One of the great things about a casino is that people feel they can relax there and forget daily life for a time. The thoughts we might have there are infinitely different from those we might need in order to understand the string quartets of Shostokovich, or the impact that Stravinsky's Rite of Spring had on subsequent generations of composers. I'm not attempting to trivialise what people discuss in their social time. Not at all. But many people have difficulty with the idea of putting themselves in the shoes of a mythological hero (composer, conductor, performer) in order to benefit from the wisdom and experience of our ancestors—because it's something we're out of touch with in contemporary society. Just as art can enable us to see the world differently for the duration of a play or a concert, the casino experience can allow us to forget that we live in a crappy flat for which we pay too much, or that we only have $187 left in our account until payday.

The title of this chapter is taken from an excellent essay, 'The Cathedral and the Bazaar', in which Eric Steven Raymond examines two opposing development systems used in the creation of software. In particular, he looks at the development of the Linux operating system and how the method of its creation challenged many assumptions about the way software should and could be effectively built. He highlights one of many of the unanticipated impacts of the internet: that not only can it be a tool for us to deliver information at the touch of a button to more people than before, but also that a virtual environment can develop and sustain its own highly effective culture completely outside accepted paradigms of thinking and working.[11]

If we were willing and able to build a structure that had at its heart a way of working that connected us to the core of mainstream Australian values, and acknowledged the real sources of our emotional and intellectual lives, if we then added to it everything else that the arts sector is able to provide, including discussion, inspiration, imagination, flexibility, risk taking and pushing boundaries—what might then be possible? A good starting point might be to ask people more, and different, questions about classical music.

4

New day

For my tenth birthday my father gave me Dale Carnegie's *How to Win Friends and Influence People*. An odd choice of gift for a child, perhaps, but one of Carnegie's principles has stuck with me: the most beautiful word in the world to other people is their name. Remembering people's names and paying attention as you are being introduced were two ideas that Carnegie proposed as starting points for building a good connection with other people.

Instead of pressing people to come and see the results of our creativity, perhaps we in the artistic community might adapt Carnegie's advice and *ask them about their own creativity*. Then, as we begin to understand the relationship that individuals have with their own creative spark, we might come to better appreciate what motivates people's interest in art. Not everyone sees themself as a tone-deaf enthusiast who likes to watch someone else do all the hard work. As was noted in a research report undertaken for the Australia Council in 2010,

> [P]eople surveyed [...] felt quite strongly that "[t]he arts should be as much about creating/doing these things yourself as being part of an audience". [...] But almost half of the people who attended music performances did so as spectators.[12]

Now that it's been part of our lives for a good fifteen years or more, we are beginning to see that the possibilities offered by the world of the internet are not simply in the exchange of information, or in being 'spectators'. New ways of behaving and interacting socially, as well as commercially, are shaping the direction of online interaction in the form of social-networking success stories including Facebook and MySpace. When it comes to sharing, commenting on and responding to art, or discovering artists, YouTube is one of the first places we might go to for information, and if we like what we see and hear the next stop might be an itunes store. On these sites you can approve or rate what you see, or you might be invited to vote in online competitions or contribute a line on Twitter. But what is interesting about the internet and the explosion of interest around certain communities is that the conversation taking place there is not always particularly sophisticated and interaction is often limited to simple tasks that require a little button-clicking and not much in the way of deep thought. Blogs, one could argue, are the place where more serious discussion might take place, within communities of like-minded people. For the purpose of this essay, however, I'm interested in looking at where most people are, regardless of whether they've read a classical music-related blog or not.

The internet offers us two significant opportunities: first, to ask people what they think about classical music and how a performance might be made more involving or more interesting; and second, to provide something more inclusive than the present diet. If we were able to offer great, original content, and invite interaction via the internet that asked a different kind of question, we might sow seeds for future music lovers simply by asking them to contribute their thinking.

It's not hard to see why this way of approaching things might horrify the classical-music specialist. It momentarily puts the power in the hands of a consumer who knows much less about the repertoire than we do, someone who might be clear about the music they know but nervous about what they don't know and unsure how much it might appeal to them. But it's also about putting the power in the hands of people with whom we don't normally engage. We're not very good at talking to those who are not already classical-music lovers, and for too long we have been uninterested in what they might have to say. I'm not suggesting that we stop talking to our traditional following but we already know their likes and dislikes. And we know that there aren't enough of them to sustain us. We need more friends, and they need to come from those places within our community in which we are not currently looking.

As a sector we might begin looking in a couple of different directions. The first is to our immediate community, which may not consist of like-minded people, but will be people with whom we come into regular contact. We need to rethink our attitude in the way we interact with them. The second is more radical: by looking to develop completely new audiences by putting the classics into their hands.

Being a good neighbour
Case study: Brooklyn Academy of Music

In 2009, as part of a Churchill Fellowship project to investigate the positive impact the arts was making in communities worldwide, I interviewed more than 120 people. Among these were three passionate people working at the Brooklyn Academy of Music (BAM) in New York. A number of things struck me about these particular interviews, not least of which was the high level of responsibility the organisation took for its role as a 'big fish' in the Brooklyn artistic community.

As stated on its website, 'BAM's mission is to be the pre-eminent progressive performing and cinema arts centre of the twenty-first century'. Established in 1861, it is America's oldest continuously operating arts centre. Its innovative, cutting-edge mainstage program of more than 220 performances attracts more than half a million people annually and features a range of nationally and internationally renowned artists. The BAM centre also houses a cinema, restaurant and bar.

BAM is an excellent example of being connected at every level of activity—inside and outside the organisation. My interviews with staff-members in three different departments reflected the cohesiveness of the organisational mission in both intention and execution.

'The social agenda and building relationships are critical to the aims of the marketing department', said Vice-President of Marketing and Communications, Lisa Mallory—but still not without hazards. The first time I visited BAM it was quite a challenge to work out where to go upon exiting the subway: as Lisa explained, new signage was in process of being developed. Rather than simply taking care of its own interests, the Academy had invited their smaller neighbours to have the street directions to their studios included as part of the signage, at BAM's cost. People exiting the subway now have a great sense of a vibrant artistic neighbourhood, which benefits everyone, and BAM shares the benefits of its size (which includes a greater share of limited resources) with its local community of artists.

BAM's education program is not typical children's programming; it features the same content as their mainstage program, which is designed for adults. Care is taken to ensure that young people have a positive and meaningful encounter with the shows on offer, without diminishing the experience. Every school that attends a show receives a visit from a teaching artist at BAM who gives a pre-show preparation workshop aimed at engaging the students, particularly with productions of quite sophisticated content. As Suzanne Youngerman, who directs the Department of Education and Humanities, explained:

> Part of the ethos is to do challenging work and perhaps create a generation of little challengers. We are trying to offer stimulating cultural experiences to public school kids who don't have many resources and are very narrow in their experiences. Most kids' lives are focussed around their own block,

and they are not highly mobile. There is not much happening in terms of arts in schools. The kids are mostly African American; they don't think they are welcome, or it is not part of their parents' experience, or they don't have the economic resources.

BAM also undertakes responsibility for these 'little challengers' beyond their involvement in BAM programs. The Academy started a college scholarship program five years ago with two prerequisites: applicants must have completed a BAM program and must be a theatre or dance major. In other words, there is a clear sense here of a longer-term approach being taken to supporting an interest in the arts.

Tammy McGaw, BAM's Director of Government and Community Affairs, believes that the Academy holds a unique position in its neighbourhood. With public housing existing alongside multi-million-dollar condo developments and residents who have been out-priced in Manhattan, their neighbourhood is a diverse one, including artists, African Americans and people of all ages. McGaw's role demands that she ask what BAM does to serve its community and whether it is being a good neighbour. This is reflected in a number of ways. In 2009, it stretched from community consultation and planning input for the Muslim Voices Festival to ensuring that all of their frontline people for that event—ushers, coat checks etc.—had been counselled in cultural sensitivity with regard to Muslim traditions and values. 'Meaningful engagement comes from the idea of where we fit into someone's life', explained McGaw:

> It is easy for an institution to be an island, but diverse audiences make a big difference and make for a more dynamic experience. It goes back to the

idea of what is in your DNA and the DNA of the organisation. It is important for people to try to bring about change in bigger institutions where you have more impact. It is important for BAM to be part of people's lives.

How might we in Australia learn from this example? BAM acknowledges that they have a bigger slice of the resources pie than others, and they behave accordingly, both in their thinking, and their actions. They are also consistent in the way they share with other artists, certain stakeholders and their immediate community. Perhaps we could establish partnerships between music-making organisations of all shapes and sizes to pool resources in order to realise a work. Perhaps large well-funded organisations and performing-arts organisations might offer more support to smaller community music clubs by allowing these clubs to handbill at concerts, or provide them with a page of free advertising in their glossy concert programs, made available on a first-come-first-served basis, to draw attention to other classical music events in the area.

Activities and gestures of this kind would demonstrate a willingness and ability on the part of separate organisations in the music sector to collaborate for their mutual benefit and to communicate a picture of the sector as a whole. If we want people to see how integral classical music is to a healthy society, and how important it is in ours, we need to do more than write about it in our grant applications, or include it in the mission statements on our websites. We need to demonstrate it with our actions.

5

You have to break eggs to make an omelette

Case study: The Polyopera project

In February 2008, Stephen Phillips, CEO and Artistic Director of the State Opera of South Australia, itemised the strengths and weakness of opera in the following way. Its strength, he wrote, is that it is

> one of the greatest of all theatrical art forms combining drama, the visual arts and music into a powerful and often deeply emotional theatre experience. Opera is unique in that it has the extraordinary ability to suspend the audience's disbelief in a way that no other performance art form can.

But its weakness, which Phillips believed to be 'a major issue facing all Australian opera companies', was audience development:

> With most companies presenting mainly standard repertoire in traditional productions, there is little to attract younger generation audiences. Development of the art form through the creation of new works and reinterpretations of existing classics may provide opportunities to build audiences.[13]

When I returned from my 2009 Churchill Fellowship I decided to establish a company that would focus on the idea of transformation through collaboration, i.e. the development of artistic projects in which people were encouraged to talk about their ideas and feelings on all manner of topics and then to turn the results of these discussions into an art work. The aim was to enable the people involved to look with fresh eyes at themselves, their ideas and feelings and, of course, different art forms themselves. My underlying reasoning was simple: if a person didn't value their own creativity, why would they value that of somebody else?

The company I established was Polyartistry, a creative ensemble of individuals who came with a background in experimental works involving audiences and communities. Drawing on the unique skill-set of its members, Polyartistry's works are platforms for large-scale creativity aimed at getting people to take one step outside themselves, underlined by a multi-disciplinary approach to generating engaging experiences for people that connect them with ideas, concepts and their surroundings.

It seemed to me that here in Australia, when we tried to develop audiences for classical music, we did so on the assumption that a traditional appreciation of the art form was already firmly in place. All we had to do was to let people know that the concert was on. That approach might have been successful if you were targeting an existing audience, but it doesn't really work when you are trying to attract new people whose view of what constitutes art and culture might be vastly different from our own. In search of his reaction to these thoughts, I spoke with the Artistic Director of Opera Australia, Lyndon Terracini, who agreed:

In terms of talking about creativity within major performing-arts organisations, particularly classically-based organisations, people are extremely creative within those forms but I think they are often not connected to how they can use technology to amplify their creativity. Very often within the classical forms, the people who are referred to as the creatives are not connected well enough with contemporary forms of creativity.

The Australia Council report, *More than Bums on Seats*, took up this issue last year and provided an interesting perspective:

Australians more readily associate the arts with individual benefits (such as a form of expression, inspiration and personal growth) than community benefits (such as understanding others and feeling a part of the community). Many people attend the arts primarily as a social occasion and in response to requests to attend by their family and friends, rather than for the art form itself.[14]

A remarkable 89 per cent of those interviewed about the positive value of the arts believed that the arts 'expose us to new ideas and get us to question things'.[15]

One in three Australians are already using the internet for the arts—mostly for attendance-related activities [...], but some are using it for creative participation (such as posting works of art, writing blogs or working with others to create art). [...] More than half of all 15–24 year-olds had used the internet to engage in some form of art during the last year and were more creative online than others. The most widespread online art creations are writing and visual art/film/video, while the most frequent mode of creative participation is being involved in an online community or social network concerned with art in some way. [...]

Creators are more likely to be:

- 15-24 years
- Highly engaged: both participating and attending
- Attending Indigenous arts
- High-school or tertiary students
- Really like the arts.[16]

The report found that young people 'displayed higher levels of creative participation than the rest of the population.

> They were more likely to be creatively engaged in visual arts and crafts, theatre and dance, creative writing and music. This was to some degree a reflection of education; with young students more active in creative participation than young workers. Arts participation levels amongst younger people also appeared to be on the rise, with this group more likely to have increased their involvement in the arts in the last year. With a higher concentration of internet users, young people were engaging with the arts in new and evolving ways.[17]

The 2010 report confirmed my belief regarding the value, the social and artistic benefit, of the sort of work Polyartistry could undertake, so we proposed to Opera Australia a collaboration, the Polyopera project. In addition to myself as musician and curator, our creative team comprised playwright David Finnigan, filmmaker Sarah Kaur, designer Matthew Aberline, and a network of associate artists that included director Laura Scrivano, composer Carlos Lopez Charles, the experimental theatre collective Applespiel, composer Drew Crawford, musicians Bobby Singh (tabla), Sarangan Sriranganathan (sitar), Rima aka Soul beats (MC); hip-hop beats producer and composer Morganics, and DJ JayTee. Polyartistry offers multiple entry points and reference points in their installation-based projects that give a wide range of participants an equally wide range of engagement. But the starting point is always the same: What do you think about ... ?

All theatre is a risk, and it is to Lyndon Terracini's great credit that he was prepared to accept our proposal and see it as a challenge. He said:

> This is the first time in its entire history Opera Australia has ever done anything like this. [...] With something like this you are investing in a possibility. You can't know what the outcome is going to be, but it is important for creative organisations to take a risk and to experiment, and that's what this is about. It's also important to do it out of your comfort zone.

So, Polyopera went ahead: Polyartistry and Opera Australia worked together to produce three short video operas, which were created and released throughout June 2011. Constructed around creative contributions from target communities and the general public, our aim was to bring opera to life by asking people to get involved in the making of it.

We chose three operas from the Opera Australia winter season—Puccini's *La Bohème*, Mozart's *Don Giovanni* and Delibes' *Lakmé*—and one aria from each. These became the source of musical material for each mini-version. The Polyartistry team worked with partner organisations, the general public, specific community and artist groups and different departments within Opera Australia to create three live events and a number of online activities that had a strong focus on people participating by giving their opinion or making a creative contribution.

The project's ambition was to engage the general public with artists as creators of opera. Those who might never have known about the art form could become involved in a range of real and virtual ways. The structure of the project directly challenged existing preconceptions of opera by incorporating into the presentation elements of popular musical culture and exploring other contemporary performance settings. The final operas reflect these influences beautifully and effectively in myriad ways.

La Bohème: Bohemian Deconstruction reworked the 1896 opera, transferring the action from nineteenth-century Paris to the funky Surry Hills loft space that is by day the home of Curiousworks, an organisation dedicated to helping new Australians tell their stories. It featured a deconstruction of Mimi's aria by Sydney-based composer Drew Crawford with a libretto by David Finnigan using contributions he received via Twitter. The audience, if they wished, could dress up in the Bohemian costumes provided, enjoy a glass of mulled wine and spend time being a bit bohemian themselves—contributing poetry and drawings to our Sydney Wall of Bohemia, playing with our fridge-magnet poetry, telling stories in our 'confession lift' and participating as extras in our film shoot. Opera Australia soprano Taryn Fiebig, as the tragic consumptive Mimi, sang her death scene surrounded by the audience, all holding candles.

Don Giovanni Remixed (aka The Don) was a marriage of opera and hip hop in which Opera Australia's baritone Tom Hamilton, as Don Giovanni, went head-to-head with a very angry Donna Elvira performed by Rima (aka Soulbeats). If you want to know who won, you'll have to check out the YouTube video, where you can be the judge. The fusing of Mozart's late-eighteenth-century opera with a hip hop soundtrack crafted by Morganics, DJ JayTee and Soulbeats drew the subject matter—love and revenge—firmly into twenty-first-century popular culture. Graffiti and street culture were woven into the design of the set and the interactive opportunities offered: a graffiti artist worked with us to build and decorate huge inflatable blocks that filled the performance space, and at the performance graffiti sent by the general public via the internet were projected, along with rhymes for the battle (yes, there was a battle in our version!) that people had tweeted to us. In Blacktown a standing, dancing, cheering and clapping audience created an atmosphere utterly foreign to that usually observed in the opera theatre or concert hall. Moreover, in hip hop, that kind of interaction is fundamental to the overall energy and feel of the performance and the audience understands that they have a vital part in sustaining that. Where else could we possibly go to a classical music performance that held a BBoy or beat-boxing workshop prior to the show, and a jam and a dance-off during the performance? Our classical art forms might think seriously about borrowing a few ideas from hip hop.

The final reworked opera, *Lakmé: Parramatta Imaginings*, explored the cultural layers of the Lakmé story, set in nineteenth-century India under British rule, through the incorporation of Indian classical music and contemporary electro-acoustic music. The contemporary youth dance company, YouMove, who are based in Parramatta, created a choreography of Bollywood-inspired movement that was taught to the audience at the performance and filmed for our video. The outside walls of the Parramatta Park Bathhouse were decorated with thousands of paper flowers made in advance and on the day of the performance with the help of volunteers. The outdoor park setting generated a lot of interest from passersby who don't usually stumble upon an opera film session in progress in the course of their Saturday walk in the park.

The Polyopera project laid considerable emphasis on popular platforms for socialising and interacting online (opinion-based, low-level creative engagement ranging to highly individual, high-quality artistic work) as its basis. None of these other art forms or methods of presentation or access are commonly associated with opera.

So how else did we use the internet in this exploration of opera?

We were anxious to share as widely as possible our process of creating the work. For people who are not actually participating in what we are doing this can be one of the most interesting aspects of our work; but we don't always think of displaying it. So, throughout the project, a blog closely tracked our activities, documenting each stage of production and providing a platform for creative contributions through a variety of off-the-shelf social-media programs. We formed partnerships with other organisations that had platforms for discussion about and engagement with the project, including ABC Classic FM and the New Music Up Late program, and the Australian Music Centre through its blog and online journal. Our venue partners, Curiousworks, Parramatta Parks Trust and Blacktown Arts Centre, helped in the sourcing of space, equipment and other performers, and broadcast details of our live performance events to their networks.

The online activities gave the audience/creator a variety of ways in which to become involved. There were simple, tick-a-box responses (indicating dis/approval on our Facebook page), and more complex activities that required more time and concentration. These included uploading images, sharing stories and drawings, and, as we've already seen, tweeting us libretto for *La Bohème* and ideas or rhymes for *Don Giovanni*. But most importantly, we just got out and asked the public what they thought about opera. We launched the project concept in Sydney in April, through two vox-pop sessions at the Sydney Entertainment Centre Forecourt and Circular Quay, where we set up an installation with Persian rug, chaise longue and a range of Opera Australia costumes for people to try on and be photographed wearing. While they were imagining themselves as another Sutherland or Tahu Rhodes, we gathered and recorded their views on opera.

Interestingly, hardly any of the people we spoke to had ever attended the opera. On the other hand, not one said that they hated it, and they were genuinely delighted to have the chance to try on a costume, and not only be photographed by us but also by one another. Instead of lecturing people on opera, being experts talking down to novices, we managed to create one-on-one conversations through a wide range of activities and possibilities for engagement. As a result our audiences were most unusual for opera. As Terracini acknowledged:

> The obvious things that come from these kinds of projects are that you will see very different people in the audience from what you see in the opera theatre. The people who engage with it online will

> be a different audience again [...] It's about building
> blocks on a long pathway that lead you to something
> else [...] and if it does suddenly become like the
> chookie dancers, then that's terrific.

The Polyopera project as a whole was very much
centred on the idea of putting opera where people
would least expect to find it, as a way of contacting
people who might have had little or no previous
connection with the art form—perhaps an annual
attendance at Opera in the Park?—or have had a
different cultural upbringing from our own. It's a
critical step. When we consider that most classical
music reflects Western European ideas and values, we
can see that we have some work to do. This is backed
up by research prepared for the Australia Council:

> Sixty per cent of non-participators and 49 per cent
> of non-attendees were not interested in engaging.
> The qualitative research found the lack of exposure
> to the arts was a major barrier to arts participation.
> For people to have an interest in the arts they must
> have participated, usually from an early age. Clearly,
> the role of education and/or parents is critical to
> experiencing the arts as a child, but increasingly
> the internet offers a convenient way to explore the
> arts at any age.[18]

Often when we develop ideas like Polyopera, or seek
funding to make them possible, we are required to
shoehorn ideas and concepts that are difficult to
quantify into measurements that don't suit artistic-
practice-as-research projects. What is the long-term
value of starting an individual conversation with
someone about classical music? Is this of greater or
lesser value than the bum-on-seat of a person who
already knows about classical music? For a long time

we have been focussing on getting people to come to our concerts, without taking the time to develop interesting, artistically sound, alternative options for people who are not engaging with us. It's a mark of the Polyopera project's success that one in two of the people who interacted with us did so online. This provided a framework in which showing up to a live event was one part of the package, but another, and critical, part was the discussion that went on before and after the performance.

Readers who would like to see something of our work with Puccini, Mozart and Delibes, and hear the reactions of those who participated in the Polyopera, may do so by visiting the web sites listed at the end of this essay.

6

Double deafness

Classical musicians might argue that the issues that influenced different composers at certain periods in their career are much the same as those that affect our lives today. Opera lovers might tell you that the plot of an opera is every bit as implausible as those we enjoy in a contemporary television soap opera. But there are equally major differences, of course. For a start, this music is no longer the popular music of the day, and the internet has brought about a revolution in popular culture. Relevance is not necessarily our biggest problem: being heard at all is a far greater challenge.

Two factors that threaten our enjoyment are what Hugh Mackay refers to as 'the need for constant buzz', and an increasing lack of discrimination about the quality of the information that confronts us:

> The need for constant buzz is like an addiction, and it has some interesting effects on us. Not only do we crave instant reactions, instant responses and instant gratification, but we expect everything to be stimulating—to amuse us, distract and entertain us. Television might have led the way, but the whole IT revolution [...] reinforces the idea. Whether it's education, politics, religion or current affairs, we need pace, colour and movement; we are in constant need of something else [...] If we don't have time to weigh, assess, reflect and interpret the information cascading over us, how can we become wise? Might we lose our sense of which bits are relevant?[19]

In this context it is difficult as a sector to respond to the kind of complex challenges faced by classical art forms: how to explain the historical sources of our repertoire and the way in which these relate to current social and environmental factors. Which brings us back to: How do we get around that clash of realities between a tokenistic attitude towards what we do to get the funding/sign off on the acquittal, and what we do because we really, deeply mean it? If we love and believe in what we are doing, then how can we meaningfully connect with the people at the casino to see if they might check out the cathedral once in a while?

I believe the rhetoric that all Australians should have access to both our classical heritage and the living traditions of new music, and that art should have a place in daily life. I also realise, so long as we who work in classical music maintain and honour as our highest form of thinking the viewpoint of the specialist alone, that this simply isn't possible. There is an enormous divide between, on the one hand, what might be perceived as an elitist way of thinking, and on the other, what it takes to create an environment that offers people equal intellectual and emotional opportunity to understand and enjoy classical art forms.

Our recent cultural-policy history has driven the classical-music sector further into the need to specialise—except that now we are required to have numerous other specialisations such as business skills, or grant-writing ability or marketing and self-management skills, in addition to our music making. We are working ourselves into a frenzy of reporting, documentation and marketing in addition to investing taxpayer's money to fund costly administrative machinery—and without really understanding why we are building the machine, or what it is required to do in a more global sense.

If we were to propose constructing a mechanism for sharing music, then most classical musicians would want one in which they can do their part without distraction, because their work requires absolute concentration. Thinking about how to attract an audience, or develop or maintain one, does not usually reside in the same headspace as rehearsal mode. Similarly, people working in administration are concentrating on their section, refining and fine tuning it, going through similar processes as are the other departments. This creates a cycle of extensive reproduction and limited cooperation, all worrying about achieving stellar results, often to the point of losing sight of the purpose of their collective existence. In other cases there are artists trying on their own to maintain an out-of-date machine that is constantly breaking down. An enormous amount of time, energy and money goes into discussing, refining and reporting on processes that are unseen by the general public and often have no impact on their lives, or getting our arts to be part of that equation. The government says to the classical music industry, 'Perhaps we need to change the specifications a bit, and you'll need to bring the motor in every year or two for inspection.' What does the average Australian say? 'I'm saving up for a Holden V6 with all the options.'

7

Opportunities

Most of us in the classical music sector, however, are unable to understand what it is that separates us from the average Holden driver, and so have no real idea how to address the problem. It's not the fault of the sector as a whole, or of us as individuals; it just reflects a general trend in our society over the last decade, something upon which Hugh Mackay has commented:

> We are world champions at creating a harmonious society from a blend of people who, over the years, have come here from every imaginable birthplace.

> That suggests tolerance should be a cardinal virtue in the Australian character, but that's a pretty feeble contender for a defining value: who wants to be merely tolerated? Aren't we overdue for a bit more healthy curiosity about each other? Isn't it time to develop a heightened respect for difference, alongside our natural affinity with people who are like-minded? [...] Then we'll start to realise that diversity—in a society as in an ecosystem—breeds strength, and homogeneity is bad for us.[20]

The cultural policy, *Creative Nation*, and the subsequent influence of a way of structuring arts funding and administration around twin opposing poles of artist and appreciator, seem to have set in place behaviour that has only limited effectiveness when it comes to building a role for classical music in the daily life of Australians. It remains a niche-market activity, reserved for a select group of people with a specific educational and economic profile. That would be fine, except that this seems to be at odds with at least one of the aspirational goals of *Creative Nation*, namely the ideal of democratic access to excellent art for all Australians. We find echoes of this in current cultural-policy documents. We also seem to have difficulty finding ways to connect with a broader range of people. The reason for this is clear enough, however: we often look to the wrong people for answers; we survey people who already come to see our work and we value the viewpoint of the expert without pausing to consider whether we might actually be wrong or out of touch, and that someone else might have a better solution. Just as Hugh Mackay insists that we should do better than basic tolerance, so being 'business-like' within our own institutions, large or small, is not really the defining value for which we should be striving.

Major performing arts organisations might learn a lot from engaging more with individual, freelance artists. It is very difficult to be responsive and flexible in an administratively heavy, hierarchical work environment. Size shouldn't be an excuse for not being able to try new things: we could all benefit from adopting a point of view that incorporates our role in the historical traditions of classical music under the heading of 'history-in-the-making' as well as preserving traditions from the past. Finally, we have a lot to learn from people who are currently not engaging with us, and by connecting with them finding new ways of sharing classical music. That is not a hard conversation to initiate, if we start from the perspective of what we all have in common: an inner creative spark that might express itself through a beautiful performance, just as it might be glimpsed in the way someone does their hair, creates a photo album on Facebook or selects songs for their ipod. It's possible to be a player and, at the same time, a fan of classical music: 'I don't think being in a band means you stop becoming a fan of the music that got you there,' writes Kerry King of Slayer. 'I'm in Slayer and I'm a fan of Slayer. I'm a fan of AC/DC, and that's never changed.'[21]

All of us who love classical music had an introduction to it that opened our ears to its fascinating possibilities in a highly personal way. If we are seriously aiming for democratic access to arts of the highest quality, including classical music, then it is vital we create fans, and opportunities for people to become fans. It's not a matter of simply putting on a good concert, nor of ensuring that every primary-school child receives concert experiences during their early years. The belief that for children to grow up to be fans of classical music they simply need to be introduced to it as part of a formal education program doesn't necessarily hold true. Most of the reasons people give for attending arts experiences are social, not educational. Indeed, this was a key factor in a company like Polyartistry's decision to go out and talk to people on social platforms. Classical music needs to find ways to embed itself in the social spaces of contemporary society. I'm not suggesting there is anything inherently reprehensible about concert halls, for it was halls of this sort that much of the classical repertoire was created. But this is not where most people are to be found these days. Modern equivalents of such gathering places include virtual environments like Facebook and Youtube. This needs to be acknowledged and respected, if we want to be listened to with the same kind of love as that with which we play.

Let me be clear: this is not another paper about how we should 'harness the internet'—it's an impassioned plea for making a greater effort to apply our tremendous creativity to different ends in which classical music might find a place for itself in the daily lives of more Australians. That requires taking our art form into new contexts, where people very different from regular Opera House patrons can be encountered and introduced 'up close and personally' to the way in which classical music is made. It is something it would be wise for us to undertake— intelligently, sensitively and willingly,

At the same time it has to be said that today in Australia, the paradigm of the classical music artist performing to an appreciative but small audience is losing its validity. Some music lovers will always retain their interest, but there is potential for many more people to take an interest in hybrid versions of this formula, with some reference to past traditions. The problem is that we are afraid of exploring these in case we don't get the artistic stamp of approval. In case it might somehow be seen as an admission of failure. Is it heresy even to suggest such a thing? I know that my interest in playing in tune, with the highest possible level of accuracy and expression, isn't diminished by considering other ways, better ways perhaps, of communicating with people about classical music as part of the necessity of maintaining my individual practice as an artist.

Nor is it a matter of 'educating' the uninitiated into the 'deep mysteries' of classical music. People don't need to be 'more educated' about classical music. They know what they are interested in. In order to reconcile the tension between creator and appreciator, in order to realise some of the aspirations of cultural policy documents such as *Creative Nation*, in order to prevent the classical sector from becoming increasingly marginalised in a highly competitive environment, we need immediately to reframe both our approach and our way of communicating to the general public.

I am not calling for a stop to be put to all traditional teaching of classical music education. But I am urging that this education be undertaken in a more imaginative way, for adults as well as young people. In this regard we are missing some important steps on our pathway to engagement. The first is just that—engagement—getting people listening to, thinking and talking about classical music in the first place. The second might be to offer them an experience they might enjoy, that might be 'ear-opening' in some way. And the third might be to have them take positive action like purchasing a ticket and attending a concert. As long as we continue to neglect steps one and two, we are hampering our own efforts—but at the moment, most of the energy seems to be concentrated on step three.

Classical musicians, and people working in the classical music field generally, are guardians of a magnificent and powerful human tradition that is full of beauty, imagination, deep thinking, aspiration and all those things that might help us to think at a level beyond daily survival. In contemporary Australia, most of us, given the security and affluence in which we are fortunate enough to be living, should be thinking well above that level. And perhaps we are. But as musicians it's up to us to start conversations that open pathways into our world, rather than expecting others to do all the work and come to us. We need to do away with the tension between creator and appreciator that has been a thread running through the history of classical music and was woven into the *Creative Nation* document, whose legacy still shapes key aspects of our major performing-arts organisations. The great thing about having a relatively small audience for the work that we do is this: we don't have much to lose in terms of experimentation, because we are aiming to access a new group of people. Frankly, any level of achievement is a positive result. This requires an acknowledgement on the part of funding bodies that if broader community engagement is to be anything more than tokenistic box-ticking, true experimentation will need to be possible and welcomed—even if initial outcomes fail to live up to expectations. We all—those of us who work at creating, promoting, funding our art form—need to follow Lyndon Terracini's lead and be prepared to take a risk. After all, isn't that what we are asking those who have never encountered classical music before to do?

****

The web sites referred to in this essay are as follows:

www.youtube.com/users/polyopera (for the work of Polyopera);

http://on.fb.me/ieKCVK (for *La Bohème: Bohemian Deconstruction*);

http://on.fb.me/iStNIA (for *Don Giovanni Remixed (aka The Don)*; http://on.fb.me/lqS1BS (for *Lakmé: Parramatta Imaginings*).

Endnotes

1   Hugh Mackay, *Advance Australia ... Where?* (Sydney: Hachette Australia, 2007), p.137.

2   *Creative Nation: Commonwealth Cultural Policy* October 1994. Introduction at http://www.nla.gov.au/creative. nation/intro.html (accessed 13 August 2011).

3   Ibid.

4   Ten artists or artistic commentators were invited to form the advisory panel to *Creative Nation*. They were Gillian Armstrong AM, Thea Astley AO, Rodney Hall AM, Jennifer Kee, Jill Kitson, Michael Leslie, Graeme Murphy AM, Bruce Petty, Leo Schofield and Peter Spearritt. They debated the matters to be contained in the policy document but did not compose it. (http://www.nla.gov.au/creative.nation/preamble.html).

5   S. Encel and M. Berry, eds *Inequality— Selected Readings in Australian Society, and Anthology* (Melbourne: Longman Cheshire, 1987), pp.120-1.

6   *Creative Nation*, p.7.

7   Anthony Bozza, *Why AC/DC Matters* (New York: HarperCollins, 2009), p.112.

8   *Why AC/DC Matters,* p.112.

9   Mackay, pp.253–4.

10   Mackay, pp.254, 266.

11   Eric S. Raymond, *The Cathedral and the Bazaar*, (Thyrsus Enterprises, 2000), p.3. ESR@THYRSUS. COM.

12   *More than Bums on Seats: Australian Participation in the Arts*, a report commissioned by the Australia Council (Sydney: Australia Council, 2010), p.7.

13 Phillips, Stephen, *The Music Council of Australia's SWOT Analysis of Opera* (Sydney: Music Council of Australia, 2008.) At www. musicforum.org.au/.../ index.php?tittleswot_analysis_of_opera (accessed 7 August 2011).

14 *More than Bums on Seats*, p.5.

15 *More than Bums on Seats*, p.31.

16 *More than Bums on Seats*, p.6.

17 *More than Bums on Seats*, p.7.

18 *More than Bums on Seats*, p.23.

19 McKay, pp.127–9.

20 McKay, p.159.

21 Bozza, p.116.

Did You Know?

- PLATFORM PAPERS are now available on line electronically for purchase for a week, a month or to keep on your on-line bookshelf.
- A growing list of videos by our authors and public speakers are posted on our website. Check it out at http://www.currencyhouse.org.au/videos
- Hard copies are on sale as usual and may be ordered via the website or by downloading and faxing our order form. Go to www.currencyhouse.org.au/publications/papers

Are you up to date with our issues?
And with the videos that support them?

PP28: July 2011
THE FALL AND RISE OF THE VCA
Richard Murphet

The Victorian College of the Arts was founded to provide training in all the visual and performing arts within the one institution. In 2009, however, unwelcome intervention by government, fuelled by public commentary, raised a public outcry. What financial pressures began has now become a deeper struggle about the nature of arts training. This period of crisis, writes Murphet, brought to the school a new vitality and purpose, and raised questions that go way beyond the VCA case alone.

PP27: April 2011
HELLO WORLD! Performing Arts on the Web
Robert Reid

Audiences for these social media are no longer restricted to receiving information, they engage in a dialogue and publish their own content. For the performing arts community these changes present significant opportunities. The potential is infinite, writes Reid, but not without risk, including IT addiction and information overload. He highlights areas of conflict, such as copyright and intellectual property legislation, privacy and quality control, and discusses opportunities for the arts with experts in the field.

PP26: January 2011
NOT JUST AN AUDIENCE
Lenine Bourke and Mary Ann Hunter

This essay is about generation shift and how young people, children and the theatre artists who work with them are leading the demand for change. Young people get the current shift better than anyone else, say the authors: they're living it, activating it, and they're even making money out of it. What if the balance of power was reversed and young people were brought in on the act of transforming our theatre? The authors explore why and how.

FORTHCOMING

PP30: January 2012
INDIG-CURIOUS: How non-Aboriginal Performers access Aboriginal Themes
Jane Harrison

Non-Aboriginal authors are increasingly incorporating Aboriginal themes and characters into their writing. While the protocols are clear these do not always translate to performance. Some argue that it is the actor's role to use their skill to portray a character, regardless of their race, gender, age; but is it acceptable— or will it ever be— for a non-Aboriginal actor to perform an Aboriginal role? What are the barriers? And how can Aboriginal themes best be incorporated into mainstream productions?